THE GREAT DICKENS FAIR® CHARACTER COLORING BOOK

BY DON CARSON

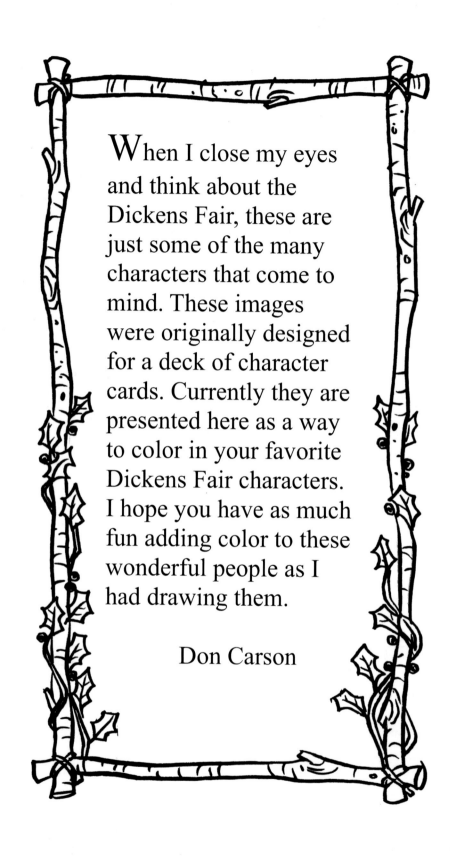

When I close my eyes and think about the Dickens Fair, these are just some of the many characters that come to mind. These images were originally designed for a deck of character cards. Currently they are presented here as a way to color in your favorite Dickens Fair characters. I hope you have as much fun adding color to these wonderful people as I had drawing them.

Don Carson

MR. DICKENS

MR. FEZZIWIG

MR. CRUMMLES

Feed
the
Puppets

SCROOGE

FATHER CHRISTMAS

PHILEAS FOGG

DR. WOLFRED BODIE

SWEEP

FLORA FINCHING

SIR MULBERRY HAWK

GHOST of CHRISTMAS PAST

GHOST of CHRISTMAS PRESENT

WINNIE-WOOPSIE TAPPERTIT

QUEEN VICTORIA

PRINCE ALBERT

PADDY WEST

MR. MICAWBER

BETSEY TROTWOOD

OBADIAH FELTRUP

MISS HAVISHAM

MR. PICKWICK

WHITE RABBIT

Made in the
USA
Columbia, SC